5-SESSION BIBLE STUDY WITH VIDEO ACCESS

LIFEMARK

VIDEOS HOSTED BY
KIRK CAMERON

BIBLE STUDY DEVELOPED BY
NIC ALLEN

Lifeway Press® • Brentwood, Tennessee

EDITORIAL TEAM

Nic Allen
Writer

Reid Patton
Senior Editor

Brett McIntosh
Associate Editor

Angel Prohaska
Assistant Editor

Jon Rodda
Art Director

Tyler Quillet
Managing Editor

Joel Polk
Publisher, Small Group Publishing

Brian Daniel
Director, Adult Ministry Publishing

ISBN 978-1-0877-8430-4 • Item 005842278

Dewey decimal classification: 306.874
Subject headings: ADOPTED CHILDREN / BIRTHPARENTS / ADOPTEES

Scripture quotations are taken from the Christian Standard Bible®,
Copyright © 2017 by Holman Bible Publishers. Used by permission.
Christian Standard Bible® and CSB® are federally registered trademarks
of Holman Bible Publishers.

To order additional copies of this resource, write to Lifeway Resources
Customer Service; 200 Powell Place, Suite 100; Brentwood, TN 37027;
fax 615-251-5933; call toll free 800-458-2772; order online at lifeway.com;
email orderentry@lifeway.com.

Printed in the United States of America

Adult Ministry Publishing • Lifeway Resources • 200 Powell Place,
Suite 100 • Brentwood, TN 37027

CONTENTS

—

SESSION 1

SESSION 2

SESSION 3

SESSION 4

SESSION 5

—

ABOUT THE AUTHORS

KIRK CAMERON (host of video sessions) is known by millions as "Mike Seaver" from the 1980s hit sitcom, *Growing Pains*. Since then, he's invested his time and energy into faith and family-focused films, television shows, and live events. These projects include *Fireproof*—the marriage-centered film that became the number one inspirational movie of the year. Kirk has also produced the documentaries, *Monumental: In Search of America's National Treasure, Connect: Real Help for Parenting Kids in a Social Media World, The Way of the Master* television series, and hundreds of live events focused on marriage, family, and parenting. Kirk's new talkshow, *Takeaways*, airs weekly on Monday nights on TBN. Recently, he's been featured in the national media for his *American Campfire Revial: 100 Day Plan*. ACR urges the family of faith to return to the principles that will bring blessing and protection to America. Kirk's newest feature film with the Kendrick Brothers, *Lifemark*, is about the value of life in the womb and the beauty of adoption. His newest documentary is *The Homeschool Awakening*. He and his wife, Chelsea, met on the set of *Growing Pains* and have been married for thirty-one years. They have six children and host an all-expenses-paid summer camp for terminally ill children and their families called Camp Firefly.

NIC ALLEN Nic Allen (Bible study developer) currently serves as the campus pastor of Rolling Hills Community Church in Nashville, Tennessee. His undergraduate work was in communications from Appalachian State University, and he holds a master's degree in Christian education from Dallas Baptist University. His heart is to see God's Word come alive in people as they mature in faith and make a difference in the world. He and his wife of over twenty years, Susan, are blessed by two high school daughters and one elementary aged son.

LIFEMARK

HOPE IS AT THE HEART OF EVERY JOURNEY

ABOUT THE MOVIE

David is a young man with the world in front of him, but at eighteen years old, there are unanswered questions about the story behind him. As a happily adopted son, he understands how blessed he is. Yet, presented with an opportunity to better understand where he came from, David leans in. What he discovers is that the mystery of his story wasn't a mystery to God, but His gracious plan all along.

Lifemark highlights the gift of adoption and the way it paints a picture of the gospel. This is a film about healing and hope. It's a portrait of choosing life and then living life to the full. No matter a person's political leanings regarding the great life versus choice legal and political debates in our generation, *Lifemark* reminds each of us that life with Christ is the only way to live. Regardless of our fear or the lack thereof, we are all invited to choose life, value life, live an abundant life, and ultimately be willing to lay down our lives.

Choose life so that you and
your descendants may live.
DEUTERONOMY 30:19

LIFEMARKMOVIE.COM

HOPE IS AT THE HEART
OF EVERY JOURNEY

KIRK CAMERON   ALEX KENDRICK   RAPHAEL RUGGERO

LIFEMARK

INTRODUCTION

The opening scene of *Lifemark* will definitely leave a mark. It will most likely elicit one of two internal reactions. Either you will witness the high stakes adventure jumping of the high school friends as invigorating and immediately research nearby places where you might quite literally dive in, *or* you'll break a cold sweat, anxiously examining how dangerous such endeavors might be.

Whether anxiety inducing or adrenaline producing, cliff jumping is something that isn't neutral. Ultimately, neither is a person's family or their story. Neither is the future. Whether we're jumping out of planes or keeping our feet on the ground, life is an adventure.

No matter how thrilling or how dangerous life gets, true security comes from salvation and that, like the very life we are given and the choices we have, is a precious gift from God. A complete understanding of the gospel includes God as the Author of life. It also includes an understanding of just how dire sin is. For the gospel to have its full impact, however, it can't only be about God granting forgiveness that leads to life; it must also be about God creating a way for wretched sinners to become beloved sons and daughters in God's family.

Enter *Lifemark*.

Based on the true story of David Scotton along with his parents (birth parents Melissa Coles and Brian Nicholas, adoptive parents Jimmy and Susan Scotton) and inspired by the documentary short film, *I Lived on Parker Avenue*, the movie featuring Kirk Cameron and Alex Kendrick is a look at life and what it means to belong.

The group study, with coordinating film clips and individual exercises throughout the week, offers a theology of salvation and an invitation to place exclusive hope in Christ. Participants will walk through foundational texts from the Scriptures and build a true understanding of adoption and what it means to be God's beloved child. Along the way, you will be challenged to write parts of your own story, past and future, knowing that your life truly is a gift from God and understanding that the way you live it can be a gift to others.

HOW TO USE THIS STUDY

The *Lifemark Bible Study* provides five lessons that can be used for group or personal Bible study. Each lesson contains four elements: Start, Watch, Engage, and three days of Personal Study. Allow forty-five to sixty minutes for the group sessions.

START. Each study begins with opening discussion questions to introduce the topic and get the conversation going. This section is designed for use in a group setting but can also be adapted for individual study. Read this section and answer the introductory questions together if you're in a group.

WATCH. The Bible study contains five short clips from *Lifemark* with a brief introduction and teaching from star and producer, Kirk Cameron. Each clip is supported by a summary of the clip and discussion questions based on the truths illustrated. Instructions to access the video sessions through the Lifeway On Demand app are located in the back of this book.

ENGAGE. This section is the primary focus of each week. Leaders should spend the majority of the group session teaching while using the verses and questions provided in this section.

PERSONAL STUDY. After attending the group session, members should complete the three days of personal study at home before the next group session. Through this personal study, group members will explore biblical content and application that support the concepts introduced in the movie clips and group discussion.

As you complete the study, you'll be asked to list and pray for others in your life who might benefit from the material. As you conclude the five sessions, you'll be encouraged to consider inviting those people God laid on your heart to join you. Living life in the gospel means inviting others to know Jesus and find life, too.

SESSION 1
ADOPTION

For through faith you are all sons of God in Christ Jesus.

GALATIANS 3:26

START

Welcome to session one of *Lifemark*. If this is a newly formed group, take a few moments to share basic introductions and get to know each other. Share the simple stuff and a few lesser-known facts, such as:

- Your name and where it came from
- Occupation or main way you spend your day
- Spouse, family, or significant relationship(s)
- Lifelong dream
- Favorite food (Don't discount this last one. It could come in handy on birthdays or if you are a group with a potluck snack rotation.)

Next, think about a significant "what if" in your life. What if things turned out differently? What if you didn't attend that school or have that roommate? What if you didn't meet that someone or move to that city?

Imagine the type of "what if" in your life that would have affected just about everything else and write that in the space provided.

Without diving too far down each narrow trail, take a few moments to move around the group, giving a chance for everyone to share at least one of the possible changes that might have occurred because of that one variable.

Everyone battles "what if" ideas in life. Some of them are related to curiosity and the wonder we have over certain decisions. Some of them are linked to regret when the choices you make bring less optimal or even sinful outcomes. Some of them offer relief because you sense the script you avoided. Regardless of the feelings invoked, each of your "what if" recollections is an invitation to trust the sovereignty of God with "what actually is" and what can be next when you focus on following Him.

As you transition to the film clip together, pray as a group and ask God to speak clearly as you seek Him in this gathering.

WATCH

To access the video sessions, use the instructions at the back of your book.

Take time as a group to view the first clip in this Bible study small group which unveils the key them of adoption present in the film. Following the clip, discuss the material using the prompt provided.

SUMMARY

Jimmy and Susan Scotton lost two young sons, John and Michael. While the details of that loss aren't shared in the movie, the reference sets the specific stage for their choosing to adopt David. Being chosen by a young birth mom, Jimmy receives the call that his son has been born and the subsequent montage of David's homecoming and early years paints a portrait of delight experienced by any adoptive or biological parent of a beloved child.

DISCUSS

Describe the emotions you noticed in Jimmy and Susan in this clip.

ENGAGE

Read Galatians 3:26–4:7 aloud in the group.

The letter to the Galatian church was written by the apostle Paul. The church or group of churches the letter addresses was established during his first two journeys and this letter was written between AD 48 and 56. The word *Galatians* could have referred to both an ethnic group (north central Asia Minor in the regions of Phrygia and Galatia mentioned in Acts 16) or a political one (southern part of the Roman Empire in a province also known as Galatia which includes other areas where Paul planted churches, that is, Antioch, Iconium, Lystra, and Derbe) making exact geography a puzzle. Galatians is one of Paul's earliest letters and came in response to a false gospel being preached in the region that was causing the young believers to stumble.

> **According to verse 26, what allows us to be sons and daughters of God?**
>
> **Describe what it looks like to come to God through faith in Christ.**
>
> **What are the hallmarks of being the child of a loving and benevolent father?**
>
> **What privileges do we enjoy as sons of God?**

Spiritually speaking, all of us begin life as orphans. We have been born into a sinful world with a sinful nature and are in need of God's grace and adoption. Thankfully Paul tells us "through faith you are all *sons* of God in Christ Jesus" (3:26). Those of us who have realized we are spiritual orphans and appealed to God's grace now relate to God as *sons*. Paul's language here is intentional. In the ancient world inheritance and family privilege passed through the father to the firstborn son. Through Christ we have become sons of God. All the rights and privileges of a first born son belong to us.

This week, in your personal study, you'll discover the joy God takes in being your Father. You did not earn your adoption, and you can't lose it—it is a gift of God's grace. You are God's child, not because you are worthy, but because you placed your faith in the only One who is worthy.

DAY 1

GOD DELIGHTS IN YOU

He will rejoice over you with gladness.
He will be quiet in his love.
He will delight in you with singing.

ZEPHANIAH 3:17

On a scale of one to ten, with one being nearly impossible and ten being extremely likely, how easy is it for you to believe God loves and delights in you?

1	2	3	4	5	6	7	8	9	10

Think about the ways Jimmy and Susan celebrated and received baby David. Consider for just a moment that imagery or a similar experience from your own life.

What does it look like when a parent or grandparent takes delight in or enjoys a child? Describe that interaction in the space provided.

Contextually, Zephaniah 3:17 finds itself embedded in a prophecy concerning the wickedness of God's people. And yet, in His goodness, God removes wickedness and gathers worshipers. Humble and low, yet chosen and clean, God takes pleasure in His people.

Examine each of the following phrases from Zephaniah 3:17, and write what they indicate about you and your relationship with God using the prompts provided.

He will rejoice over you with gladness.

The NASB 1995 uses the word *exult* where we read *rejoice* in the CSB. Both are translations of the Hebrew word that means to "display joy."

What does it look like to "display joy"? What might that look like in God's relationship to you?

He will be quiet in His love.

In God's family, adopted children are beloved children. English translations of this verse vary, some indicating that God, Himself, is the one being quiet. Others offer the idea of God making us quiet. Either way, the silence speaks. There is no accusation or condemnation. If God is silent, He isn't stating His case against us. Instead, He is lovingly receiving us. If we are quieted by His love, it means we owe no proof. We can bring no answer. We only need to come and rest.

What does the word *quiet* mean to you as it relates to God?

He will delight in you with singing.

Whether it's a pregnancy post, gender reveal, baby shower, or a delivery day, we're accustomed to the idea of celebration when a baby is expected. The God of this universe made you and celebrates you. In the next session, you'll be reminded that His delight isn't because you deserve it, but because He chooses it.

How does God's delight in you prompt even greater delight in you for Him?

End this session in prayer praising God and expressing gratitude to Him for loving and adopting you.

DAY 2
FAITH IS A . . .

A person blinded by pride might compose a lengthy list of everything that makes them special. Others hindered by low self-esteem might be hard-pressed to name even a few good traits they posses. One of these approaches minimize Christ's sacrifice, assuming worth based on inherent goodness, the other rejects His gift, denying the possibility of His love altogether. Both are misinterpretations of the gift of salvation.

In the space below, write down Galatians 3:26.

Underline the word or phrase in the verse that secures sonship.

Given the choice between salvation being something you earn by good behavior or something you'll never achieve no matter how hard you try, where are you most tempted to lean?

Self-worth emerges in early childhood and follows people through adolescence and into adulthood. This is the concept of being worthy, lovable, and earning affection from others. While this type of transaction works when it comes to making a team, getting a job, or joining a musical cast, the idea of unconditional love and acceptance isn't something people embrace or exhibit easily. The oldest theological heresy is that human beings can somehow earn the favor of God through their works.

Read Ephesians 2:4-9. Of all the phrases or statements Paul makes in this pivotal passage, which one stands out most to you?

Based on the passage you just read:

Did God wait for us to be lovely in order to love us?

Where does salvation come from according to Paul?

From what or who do people derive faith?

Specifically, what does Paul exclaim faith to be in verse 8?

God's affection for His people surpasses the affection of the best earthly father. God loves us because He chose to. In *Lifemark*, David didn't earn Jimmy and Susan's favor. They chose to adopt him and love him. He wasn't their son because of his character, abilities, or resume. They chose to love him and grant him a place in their hearts and home. That is God's plan of grace for His children. And by an extravagant gift of faith, He alone allows us to see, believe, and receive that home.

Think specifically of someone who wavers in faith and has rejected Jesus. What reason or reasons do they cite for disbelief? What makes God's gift of faith so hard for people to believe?

Read the verse provided below.

The Spirit himself testifies together with
our spirit that we are God's children.

ROMANS 8:16

What role does the Holy Spirit play in our sonship?

As another part of God's incredible gift, the Holy Spirit testifies and confirms a person's place in God's family. Through the Word of God and the internal witness of the Spirit, believers are assured and reminded of God's love for them not because of our godness, but because of God's sonship isn't earned but received in faith. We don't create, grow, or manage this gift, we simply receive it as a generous gift from God the Father.

Thank God for that gift today and ask Him to help you keep in balance the knowledge of where your salvation comes from.

DAY 3

DAUGHTERS & SONS & HEIRS

If you have biological children, who looks most like you and what similar traits do they possess? If you know your biological parents, answer the same question. Who do you resemble most and what traits were passed to you?

Beyond just dominant hair color or recessive eye color, there are also personality traits shared from one generation to another. Those are transmitted both in nature, the complex biology of birth, and nurture, the circumstances surrounding the way a person is raised.

Who are you most like in your family? What makes you similar?

Go back and read Galatians 3:26–4:7. Write verse 7 below.

According to Galatians 3:29, what Old Testament connection does a believer's relationship with Christ help him or her make?

Read Genesis 15:5,18-21. What did God promise Abraham in verse 5? What does God promise Abraham's offspring in Genesis 15:18-21?

Little mattered more in antiquity within a family structure than the land and inherited blessings passed from one generation to the next. Even Gentiles unfamiliar with the Abrahamic covenant would have understood generational inheritance. In this case, the blessings belong to the children of God, even those adopted into the family and not Jewish by blood.

Faith in Christ is what makes a person God's child and if a person is God's child, he or she is God's heir. For disciples of Christ, their likeness, characteristics, attitudes, behaviors, responses, values, and disciplines are all pieces of an incredible legacy.

This next question isn't an opportunity to brag, but how is the Spirit of God conforming you into the image of Christ? Where are you demonstrating the nurtured fruit of Christlike character?

This isn't an invitation to self-deprecate or abuse yourself. What in areas do you need the Spirit's help to grow in Christlikeness?

Read Hebrews 12:28-29 below.

Therefore, since we are receiving a kingdom
that cannot be shaken, let us be thankful.
By it, we may serve God acceptably, with reverence
and awe, for our God is a consuming fire.

HEBREWS 12:28-29

God promised Abraham that his children would receive land and dominion. As Abraham's seed through adoption by faith in Christ, we're benefactors of a royal kingdom and incredible blessing that we can't imagine. Before the foundation of Abraham's family, God provided the promise of inheritance. Before the foundation of the world, He provided a Son and Savior to ensure our rights as children. It is by faith that we receive salvation and by faith that we receive the eternal blessings of being God's children and heirs to His promise. We cling to grace because only grace can establish us.

Compose a prayer of thanksgiving below, expressing gratitude to God for choosing, loving, and blessing you as part of His family.

SESSION 2
SECURITY IN CHRIST

For all those led by God's Spirit are God's sons.

ROMANS 8:14

START

Welcome to the second session of *Lifemark*. Begin by visiting the individual exercises completed between group meetings. Consider the three key concepts explored this week:

- The Lord delights in His created and chosen children.
- His favor isn't due to unique human goodness, but comes as a result of His kindness.
- His promise of salvation makes us sons and daughters and also heirs in His kingdom.

Is there anything in particular that stood out this week in the individual study material? Any truth God revealed or any question He unearthed?

As an open-ended discussion starter leading up to this week's film clip, choose to share your best answer to one of the following three prompts.

1. If you could meet and ask any question of any one person— dead or alive—who would it be and what would you ask?

2. If you could ask God any question and be given an answer immediately, what would you ask?

3. If you could time travel and meet your future self, what's one question you'd like to ask?

This idea of asking a specific question of a specific someone isn't a new one. Many people have considered this question and longed for the opportunity. Related to this concept is the idea of being able to say something to someone. Perhaps it's something left unsaid or undone in a relationship that is no longer present or active. Perhaps it's a desire to say something to someone you have never or likely will never meet. Today we will consider an impactful statement David wanted to make to his birth mother, Melissa, as well as words of security David received from Jimmy.

WATCH

To access the video sessions, use the instructions at the back of your book.

View the film clip for this session together.

SUMMARY

Children who know they are adopted will have different thoughts and questions at different developmental stages. In David's case he grew up with opportunities to ask about Brian and Melissa and to learn different parts of their stories. As with most children, David likely graduated to different levels of knowledge as he matured. In this scene, Jimmy recalls a conversation he and Susan had with David when he was only eight. And he elevates it to include a concept David could understand now, at eighteen. In both instances, Jimmy offers a consistent promise that David will never outgrow.

DISCUSS

What do David's remarks about the potential of meeting Brian and Melissa indicate about him, his childhood, and family?

What is the promise Jimmy makes to David and why is that so important for anyone?

ENGAGE

Read Ephesians 1:3-14.

The church in Ephesus was planted as part of Paul's second missionary journey, chronicled in Acts 15–17. Ephesus was the multicultural, metropolitan city on the western coast of Asia Minor (modern-day Turkey) and a major thoroughfare in the Roman Empire. Paul returned there for a visit during his third missionary journey and ultimately spent up to three years there strengthening and establishing the church. Years later, from prison in Rome, Paul penned this letter to remind his friends of the gospel and encourage them to remain full of hope despite their suffering. Ephesians is full of foundational doctrines, none so explicitly rich as that of grace.

> **Summarize your thoughts about salvation based on this passage. What does it explain about Christ's work for us?**
>
> **According to verse 13, what is the pathway to salvation?**
>
> **According to verse 14, what blessings come from the Holy Spirit as a result?**

Believers in Jesus are the children of God. To borrow Jimmy's line from the film, "You will always be [His] son." Nothing can change that fact, but circumstances threaten that belief all the time. The Holy Spirit serves as an encouraging reminder of this truth.

> **How often do you need reminders from the Holy Spirit? What are the triggers in your life that invite stress and the need for God's Spirit to remind you that you are secure in Him?**

This week's personal study sessions are about security. As much as this film celebrates the beauty of adoption, highlighting the fundamental truth of choosing life, its spiritual significance is found in discipleship. As God's children and coheirs with Christ, we have unparalleled security and status. Any challenge we endure or temptation we face should pale in comparison to who and what we are. And yet, even the most confident believers struggle. You'll be strengthened and equipped this week as you are reminded of the security found in Christ.

DAY 1
LEG ONE: FREEDOM

Have you ever built a piece of furniture with legs? So many factors go into the stability of the piece. Whether it's chair designed to support a person or a table meant to hold a buffet dinner, strength matters, but it's not the only essential. Length counts too. Precision with length is the difference between having a piece that sits square or annoyingly rocks back and forth.

This week we'll be examining three "legs" of Romans 8 that provide strength, stability, and a strong foundation for the truth that we are secure in Christ—freedom, trust, and hope.

> **Read Romans 8:1-4 and summarize these verses in the space provided.**

> **How would you define the word *condemnation*?**

The Greek word translated "condemnation" in Romans 8:1 only appears three times in the New Testament, all of which are in Romans. It is more than a declaration of guilt. It's a ruling of judgment. Final judgment. Eternal punishment.

> **According to Romans 8:1, what is the key to avoiding this sentence from God?**

Lifemark presents several pictures of freedom. Biologically, David is alive because young Melissa chose life. Spiritually, Melissa is alive because she loves Jesus and God granted her grace. As a blessing, David was afforded the chance to be part of that hope in her life. Consider the two distinctions outlined in the opening verses of Romans 8. Paul describes the law of the Spirit of life and the law of sin and of death.

In the columns provided, list the parts of your life that come under each heading. Everything sinful, discouraging, selfish, and damaging goes under the law of sin and death. Everything Christlike falls under the law of life in Christ.

Law of the Spirit of Life	Law of Sin and Death

In Christ, forgiveness has been issued; punishment has passed. No matter how long your column of sin and death is, that list is canceled. No final sentence. The final word isn't final judgment but a purchased reprieve. Freedom in Christ means freedom from the threat of eternal judgment.

Read Isaiah 41:10 and then commit to memory the first few phrases provided below.

Do not fear, for I am with you;
do not be afraid, for I am your God.

ISAIAH 41:10

Our freedom comes because Christ came. There is no condemnation and no fear because of Him. Have you placed your faith and trust in Christ? Have you recognized and repented of sin and chosen the life that Jesus died to provide? The first leg of a trustworthy foundation is freedom. It's found in forgiveness. The fact that you're forgiven is what makes you Christ's. Belonging to Him means we never have to fear condemnation.

DAY 2
LEG TWO: TRUST

Continue today in your examination of the three "legs" of Romans 8. Read the verse below and underline the words that stand out to you.

> We know that all things work together for the good of those who love God, who are called according to his purpose.

ROMANS 8:28

Summarize this verse in the space provided.

What is a way this verse can and has been misinterpreted?

Understanding that the first leg of our table is the freedom that comes from forgiveness, we turn to the next part of the foundation: trust. Believing that God only does what's good is the epitome of trust.

Circle where are you on the scale of trust, with 1 being no trust and 10 being full trust.

| 1 | 2 | 3 | 4 | 5 | 6 | 7 | 8 | 9 | 10 |

When you consider the difficulties you have faced in life or the challenges you have personally witnessed other believers experience, it can be hard to understand and reconcile Paul's words. Good does not always mean easy. Good does not mean painless. Good does not mean you will always win and never sacrifice. In fact, the very essence of Christ's life involved incredible loss and the deepest of sacrifices.

Understanding Romans 8:28 means trusting God and His good plans even when they don't make sense, aren't easy, or don't rescue, bless, or provide for you in the way you had hoped. Trusting God's plans is especially difficult when they involve pain and require sacrifice. God is trustworthy, and He is God even when His plans don't align with the script you wrote for your life. Living in trust is foundational to security.

The word *good* in this verse does not simply include the idea of what is pleasant, agreeable, and joyful. It also means what is "useful." To the true believer who loves God and is called, even the most difficult situations hold the potential for joy and are useful for God's plan.

> **Go back to Isaiah 41:10. Read the verse in your Bible and consider underlining or highlighting it. Next, read the second set of clauses from the verse below. Underline what God provides in these phrases.**

> **I will strengthen you; I will help you.**

Strength and help are both great things. We need both all the time.

> **Where do you need strength?**

> **Where do you need help?**

Although prayer matters, the following exercise isn't a spot to note your friend's illness or your coworker's upcoming travel. This is a list meant to show where you, personally, need a measure of strength—where you need the help only God can provide.

> **As you close, make a list of the areas of life where it is hardest to see the good God is doing. Ask God to give you open-handed strength to let go and fully believe He does know what's best and He will provide what is good for you.**

DAY 3
LEG THREE: HOPE

The final perfectly plumb leg of our foundational piece this week is hope. Because of God's forgiveness, we are free from condemnation. Because of God's providence, we can trust Him and live according to His plan. Because of God's presence, we can hope in His love that we can never lose.

Complete Romans 8:38-39 in the space provided below.

For I am persuaded that neither _____ nor _____,
nor angels nor _____, nor things _____ nor
things to come, nor _____, nor height nor
_____,
nor any other created thing will be _____
to _____ us from the _____ of God
that is in Christ _____ our Lord.

ROMANS 8:38-39

What comes to mind when you hear the word *abandonment*? Some cases of abandonment are low stakes. Consider online shopping. Did you know that entire studies exist to understand when, where, and why customers are most likely to abandon their online shopping carts including information on how to get those potential purchasers back? Over 70% of all online shopping carts are abandoned, but nearly 50% of emailed invites to return and complete those purchases are opened and clicked through.[1]

People matter infinitely more than any potential online transaction. Sadly, as many as twenty million children worldwide have suffered abandonment. Tens of thousands are orphaned and left alone every year.[2]

That doesn't even factor in a person left in a relationship or some other context. Neglect, abuse, or abandonment are real threats or fears for countless people. When it's part of your story and has happened before, it's no wonder you begin to expect that it will happen again. At least a part of the fear birth mothers feel in forming an adoption plan is imprinting a feeling of abandonment on her child. Part of adoptive parents' reality is loving a child who may carry wounds.

While adoption is often a brave and commendable choice for birth mothers and adoptive parents, these feelings can linger and require hope and security to overcome. The same can be said of our spiritual lives. But in Christ, we have a secure hope.

According to Paul's statement in Romans 8:38-39, what can separate us from God's love?

If you have experienced abandonment or carry the weight of broken earthly relationships and/or promises, how might that translate to your ability to believe this verse?

Read Isaiah 41:10 for the third time this week. Do you have the entire verse committed to memory yet? Read the final few phrases from the verse provided here.

I will hold on to you with my righteous right hand.

Be literal for just a moment. What is required to physically hold on to someone or something? Presence, right? Romans 8:38-39 and the final clause in Isaiah 41:10 are a perfect picture of our Father who is always present. Not only does He give strength and provide help, but He never leaves. Regardless of the experiences we have had with abandonment, abuse, or neglect, those never apply to God. He is always there. And as a loving Father, He holds on to His children.

Close this week of personal study in a prayer of acknowledgement of and thanks for the freedom, trust, and hope found in Christ. Because of Christ, we can rest assured and live in security.

RECONCILIATION

But now in Christ Jesus, you who were
far away have been brought near by the
blood of Christ. For he is our peace.

EPHESIANS 2:13-14A

START

Welcome to the third session of *Lifemark*. Begin by visiting the personal studies completed by participants between group meetings.

Is there anything in particular that stood out this week in the personal studies? Any truth God revealed or question He unearthed?

Share with the group the last thing you lost that seemed to take forever to find.

Now take a moment to share one of the most significant things you have ever forgotten. Perhaps it was an address or an appointment. Let's hope it wasn't a milestone birthday or significant anniversary.

Everyone loses or forgets something from time to time. Even the most organized people—those with hardrive-like memories—might have momentary lapses and misplace keys, a wallet, and the remote control.

But there are other things we can't forget, those things we hold on to and reflect on for days and weeks into the future. This is especially true in our relationships. Thankfully the gospel message which has reconciled us to God has also given us the ability to be reconciled to others. This week's clip shows a powerful moment of reconciliation that points to the reconciliation found in the grace of God in Christ.

WATCH

To access the video sessions, use the instructions at the back of your book.

View the film clip for this session together.

SUMMARY

The first half of the movie weaves a story of past memories and present-day opportunities for David and his birth mom, Melissa, to connect. This particular clip highlights that meeting and the immediate opportunity for reconciliation and healing for all parties. It really is a family affair, and God's gift of grace takes center stage.

DISCUSS

Why is it significant in this scene that David kindly addresses both his adoptive mom and his birth mom?

What are some possible ways this first meeting between David and Melissa could have gone?

Read the verses below.

> But now in Christ Jesus, you who were far away have
> been brought near by the blood of Christ.
> For he is our peace.

EPHESIANS 2:13-14A

**How did our relationship with Jesus change our relationship
with God?**

**Consider when you were far away from God. How did that feel?
What did God do to reconcile you to Himself?**

What does it mean for Jesus to be your peace?

Read Colossians 3:12-13 below.

> Therefore, as God's chosen ones, holy and dearly loved,
> put on compassion, kindness, humility, gentleness, and
> patience, bearing with one another and forgiving one
> another if anyone has a grievance against another. Just as
> the Lord has forgiven you, so you are also to forgive.

COLOSSIANS 3:12-13

To accept one another or bear with one another means to hold up or
sustain. That is certainly on display throughout the film in David's
family. In multiple ways, it's easy to spot David's parents holding him up
and in significant moments, you can see David holding up and sustain-
ing his adoptive parents and also Melissa. David's hope in trust in Jesus
allowed him to reconcile with Melissa.

When have you been reconciled with someone? Share that process?

**Who exhibits deep mercy and compassion in your life? What can
you learn from them?**

Followers of Jesus are people of reconciliation. Because we've been
reconciled to God, we can extend that reconciliation to others because of
the peace we have through Jesus. In your personal study this week, you'll
dive into familiar texts about what it means to find lost things and God's
economy of forgiveness and reconciliation.

DAY 1
THE LOST ARE FOUND

We use the word *lost* when it comes to misplaced items: "I lost my car keys at the restaurant."

We use the word *lost* when it comes to competition: "They lost the game in overtime."

We use the word *lost* when referring to the death of a loved one: "He lost his brother last year."

We use the word *lost* to define a person who doesn't know Christ: "He's lost in sin and just can't believe God loves him."

It's a useful word but not a positive or happy one. Take time to read the three parables in Luke 15:1-24 Jesus told about lost things.

List the similarities and differences you notice between each of the stories Jesus told.

Go back and read verses 7 and 10 again. According to Jesus, what do these stories represent?

While our natural instinct might not place value on a single sheep when ninety-nine are still accounted for, Jesus's words are meant to indicate the value of every person before God. Even one lost soul is too many. One out of ten coins may not seem like much, but when you consider ten percent of an important sum like an annual wage or a significant down payment, it makes more sense. You likely know people who have felt deep pain when their stock portfolio dips even five percent. And is there anything more valuable than a child? While the sheep was wayward, he or she didn't "reject" the shepherd. The coin certainly didn't get lost on purpose. The illustration of the son is something else. He was lost, yes, but he also chose to leave.

Take a few moments to describe your own experience with spiritual lostness in the space provided. No matter your experience, all of us have experienced lostness at one point.

All people are born in a state of lostness. As sinners, we aren't lost because we haven't been found. We're lost because all of us have chosen our lostness over God. We desperately needed God to find and rescue us. Understanding just how lost we were highlights further the gift of being found.

Regardless of when you encountered and received God's gracious gift of Christ's sacrifice, the Bible is clear that great rejoicing was the result. The father in the final story is representative of God the Father in heaven. When the sheep and coin are found, it's an angelic homecoming. When the child comes home, the father hosts the party.

Pray this week that God would bring a sense of freshness to your own reconciliation to Him. Commit to praying for people in your life who need to be found.

DAY 2
ECON 101

Yesterday, we discussed different uses for the word *lost*. Here are a few more.

We use the word *lost* to describe the state of a person's forgetfulness: "He lost his marbles."

We use the word *lost* to describe fleeting affections, too. As the Righteous Brothers famously crooned, "You've lost that loving feeling."[1]

People who know how truly dire a situation is never forget to be grateful when it's resolved. The economy of forgiveness works like this: when you know how much you have been forgiven, you know how much you ought to love.

Read Luke 7:36-48.

Consider the cast of characters in this particular passage. What are the more significant details you notice about each? Jot down ideas in the spaces provided.

Jesus

Simon the Pharisee

The woman

Write Luke 7:47 in your own words.

The word *forgiven* used by Luke in this narrative is an entirely different word than the one Paul used in Ephesians 4:32. It means "to send away, to let go, to forgive, to cancel a debt."[2] While the word Paul used brings the connotation of restoration, the word Jesus used is all about removal. Consider forgiveness like the two sides of a coin where heads represents the cancellation of a deep debt and tails the blessing of reconciliation.

This is connected to the ideas of mercy and grace. Mercy can be described as the removal of debt. It's the goodness of God that withholds the punishment sinners deserve. Grace can be described as the blessings of sonship. It's the goodness of God that grants a sinner what he or she could never earn. Our reconciliation extends beyond our forgiveness and allows us not only to receive forgiveness but also to live as forgiven people who extend that benefit to others.

As believers in Jesus, we have experienced both sides of the coin and been instructed to live them out in response. Consider your coin for a moment. Although it's not possible to lose one side without the other, it is possible to neglect one side compared to the other.

> **Which is more difficult for you in relationships—letting go of a person's debt against you or restoring that person to right standing again? Explain with examples in the space provided.**

Jesus explained that a person who has been forgiven much loves much, but one who has been forgiven little loves little. It's an economic equation. The truth is that all forgiven sinners have been forgiven much. Every account in a person's life, regardless of earthly severity, is severely overdrawn. No one deserves mercy. No one can earn grace. The problem is not the degree of forgiveness but the degree of awareness. People forget the weighty cost of their sin and the high price Christ paid. People fail to love because they downplay the true nature of God's forgiveness.

> **Spend a few minutes in prayer. Examine the description you wrote of your spiritual lostness in the first personal study this week. Pour out an expression of love and affection for Jesus to the measure of His great forgiveness of you.**

COMPARE AND CONTRAST

Lifemark offers not only a look at the developing relationship between David and his birth mother, Melissa, but also Melissa's relationship with David's adoptive mom, Susan. In fact, each relationship portrayed in the movie is one complex layered relationship on top of another, just as it is in life and as it should be in community.

Describe the relationship you observed between Melissa and Susan in the clip this week.

If you were to simply assume the role of either mom, Melissa or Susan, how might you script their real-life reactions to one another? Is it as loving and kind as you saw portrayed, or can you imagine a world where other emotions and feelings come in to play? Describe those below.

Go back to Luke 15:11-23. How did the son imagine the father would feel about Him?

Why was this fear misplaced? What did the father want for the son?

It would be easy to assume Susan might feel threatened by or jealous of Melissa. David longed to meet her, and nothing could exchange or replace the biological connection the two shared. It would also be easy to assume Susan might feel overly protective of David, not wanting him to experience any potential pain or disappointment.

Additionally, Melissa had an understandable mixture of feelings waiting to meet David. She was fearful. What she didn't know was all David wanted was to be reconciled to His birth mom. She imagined the worst. He only wanted to thank and celebrate her. Since this film is based on real lives, it's safe to assume that an entire host of emotions flooded each person.

Unlike the son in the parable, no one in *Lifemark* sinned. David's family story was filled with God-honoring choices. Both Susan and Melissa made courageous choices. All they needed was reconciliation. As they were brought together, God was honored and their faith was encouraged.

How does the gospel lead us to withhold bitterness and anger and extend reconciliation to others?

Not only did both women in the movie have David, the both had each other. In the parable, the youngest son was always wanted by the father. All he desired was reconciliation. Sometimes we stop short of reconciliation with God and others because we fear their response. With God, we will always find forgiveness and restoration if we seek it. With others it is not always certain, but reconciliation is always worth pursuing. Because we have been restored to God, we can be restored to others.

Are there people you need to be reconciled to, but fear is keeping you from taking that step? What would it look like to take a step in faith toward that person?

Pray that you would not forget the feeling of being reconciled to God and that you would be willing to love others in this same way.

SESSION 4
THE IMAGE OF GOD

I will praise you because I have been
remarkably and wonderously made.

PSALM 139:14

START

Welcome to session four of *Lifemark*. Begin by reviewing the individual exercises completed between group meetings.

This week we're going to be discussing the glorious truth that all people are made in the image of God. This truth shouldn't be controversial for believers in Jesus. It is laid out for us in the opening pages of Scripture. Though the film deals with issues that have been politicized, neither the film nor the study attached to it is an exercise in politics but an opportunity to know and honor God.

Because all people are made in the image of God, all people have immense value to God, therefore they should have immense value to us as well. As we reflect on the difficult subject of abortion, we will also consider that it is possible and necessary for us to share the truth about God's view of human life in a way that is full of grace to our hearers. We are called to do so in an effort to point others to the truth of Christ and not push them away.

What are some ways we can value all people as being made in the image of God?

What does this look like specifically for unborn children?

WATCH

To access the video sessions, use the instructions at the back of your book.

View the film clip for this session together.

SUMMARY

This week's clip highlights the title of the documentary that sparked the film. "I Lived on Parker Avenue" is a direct reference to the location of the clinic where Melissa planned to have an abortion but ultimately chose to carry and grant life. David very literally lived on Parker Avenue, a place where only God knows the volume of babies whose outcome was not the same. In this scene, Melissa meets David and his parents at the location and shares with them in great cinematic, flashback detail the truth of what almost occurred.

DISCUSS

Why do you think it was important to Melissa to share that part of the story rather than let the past remain in the past?

How did David's response and Jimmy/Susan's reactions make you feel?

ENGAGE

Read Genesis 1:26-27. What does it mean for all people to be made in the image of God?

Human beings are unique among the created order. Humankind is the only created being that God made in His image and likeness. Along with that image comes intimacy. You see that pictured in the garden, but because sin is introduced, the intimacy is broken and the image is marred.

In what ways do you see the image of God valued by the world at large? In what ways do you see the image of God ignored by the world at large?

Read Psalm 139:13-16. What does this particular Psalm lead you to conclude about life and the value of it?

Based on these verses, how would you decribe God's relationship to the unborn? How is this distinct from the way our culture views the unborn?

It's easy to see why Psalm 139 is used to give biblical value to the unborn. Before a single breath, God formed. God knew. God wonderfully made. "All my days" indicates the value continues for each person across all the days they live. This means David was created in the image of God and his spared life is precious to God. It also means young Melissa was created in the image of God, and she is no less precious to God than the life she almost took.

How should the image of God impact the way we treat others?

As you continue through your personal study this week, you'll explore the value of all life and be invited to understand the unique ways living like Jesus might influence how they receive Christ. We've already discovered that there is very real, biblical value in lost things. The way we image Jesus might be the key to finding them.

DAY 1
CHOOSE LIFE

Read Deuteronomy 30:19-20.

I call heaven and earth as witnesses against you today
that I have set before you life and death, blessing and
curse. Choose life so that you and your descendants
may live, love the LORD your God, obey him, and remain
faithful to him. For he is your life, and he will prolong your
days as you live in the land the LORD swore to give to your
ancestors Abraham, Isaac, and Jacob.

DEUTERONOMY 30:19-20

**In the passage provided, underline each command word, and
complete the phrases below.**

choose _____

love the _____

obey _____

remain _____

Moses was near the end of his life and leadership. He would not be
entering the promised land along with the traveling tribes of Israel. The
commands and instructions he received from God and passed to the
people would define and govern their social, religious, and legal existence.

**What are the three ways to choose life that Deuteronomy 30:20
offers?**

Read John 14:6. How does Jesus identify Himself in this verse?

In what ways do Jesus's words in John 14:6 help plan a course of action related to God's instructions in Deuteronomy 30:19-20?

If the people followed Moses's instruction to love the Lord, worship and adoration would be the overflow. If they received Moses's instructions to obey God, complete and total trust in Him would be displayed. If they listened to Moses's instructions to remain faithful, being consistent and true would be necessary.

Of the three instructions for choosing life given in Deuteronomy 30:20, write out how natural or difficult you find each one.

To love?

To obey?

To do both with a degree of faithful consistency that strengthens your walk with Christ?

To choose Christ is to choose to fully live, recognizing and following Him as the way and the truth. Loving Jesus, obeying God's Word, and remaining faithful to Him are actively choosing His way, His truth, and His life.

Pray and ask God to help you always choose life and lead with love in a faithful manner that honors Him.

DAY 2
LIVE LIFE

Have you ever been mistaken for someone else? Who is your doppelgänger—celebrity or otherwise?

A common reason people give for not having interest in the church is hypocrisy. Many people hold an ideal image of what a faithful follower of Jesus should look like, including how they should engage the public square, interact with others, and respond to issues. When everyday behavior doesn't match that expectation, many write off Christians as hypocrites.

Truthfully, that ideal image is Jesus. The goal is to look like and live like Him. What if there was a moment when someone mistook us for Him because of the resemblance? Would that change the unbelieving world's perception?

Read Colossians 3:10-15.

> And have put on the new self. You are being renewed in knowledge according to the image of your Creator. In Christ there is not Greek and Jew, circumcision and uncircumcision, barbarian, Scythian, slave and free; but Christ is all and in all.
>
> Therefore, as God's chosen ones, holy and dearly loved, put on compassion, kindness, humility, gentleness, and patience, bearing with one another and forgiving one another if anyone has a grievance against another. Just as the Lord has forgiven you, so you are also to forgive. Above all, put on love, which is the perfect bond of unity. And let the peace of Christ, to which you were also called in one body, rule your hearts. And be thankful.

COLOSSIANS 3:10-15

In the space provided, jot down all the character traits you notice in Colossians 3:10-15. What exactly does the "new self" look like? Act like? Live like?

The opening scene of *Lifemark* features David living his best life. Risky? Certainly! Exuberant? Without a doubt! That scene is followed by many others indicating the kind of life David lives. He has incredible friends and amazing parents. He is an athlete who excels and a student who is being challenged and encouraged. His life, from the outside looking in, seems to be so well lived. Further, when he talks to his parents, teachers, teammates, friends, and eventually the parents who gave him up, you see Jesus. In his mannerisms, tone, words, and any way that counts, you can recognize parts of Colossians 3:10-15 in action.

Take a moment to celebrate a person in your life who images Jesus well. What is it that makes him or her so much like Christ? What specifically from Paul's words in Colossians 3 is easily recognizable in this person?

Which of those traits could someone likely spot in you? What from Colossians 3 is present enough in you for someone to catch a glimpse of Him?

Examine your list and note what is missing from Paul's description of the "new self" when it comes to your life. What area do you want to focus on? Where do you want to seek God's help? Write it down in the space provided and pray about that as you close this session of personal study.

DAY 3
SPEAK LIFE

Many people believe and act on the idea that we should always say exactly what is on our minds. As you may already know, biblical wisdom doesn't articulate the same ideal. Christ followers understand that there is purpose in what we say and do. There is a strong pull toward the pseudo-freedom of the "you do you" world, but the goal is (or at least should be) to do "less you" and "more Him."

Read John 3:30. Write John the Baptist's words in the space provided.

While it might be widely encouraged to embrace be one's autonomous self, Christians are called to reject this way of thinking and pursue godliness and humility like Christ. For many, going against popular logic is difficult. For others, it is natural. Going against the grain may be something you are comfortable with. Swimming upstream, standing out, and being different from the world may be something you seek and celebrate. It may even be something you are willing to fight to protect. This is where we have to remember the need for humility.

Are you more prone to go with the crowd or go against the crowd? How do either of these responses impact our walk with Christ?

Read James 3:8-9 below.

> But no one can tame the tongue. It is a restless evil, full of deadly poison. With the tongue we bless our Lord and Father, and with it we curse people who are made in God's likeness.

JAMES 3:8-9

We can't expect people to see Christ's likeness in us and desire Christ's life for themselves if we are simultaneously cursing them.

Think of some of the words you've zeroed in on during your weeks of study so far. *Kindness. Compassion. Love. Reconciliation. Unity. Gratitude.* Even knowing the clear instructions we've been given, the tongue is indeed hard to tame, regardless of who we hurt or the damage we inflict.

Consider David and Melissa in the clip this week. Remember the flashback as young Melissa entered and exited the clinic to the shouts of strangers and the cold demeanor of the doctor? Now, recall David's first words and his reaction to the decision Melissa almost made. No poison. No evil. No condemnation. No judgment. No defensive posturing. No prideful rage. Only love. Only thankfulness. Only presence and support.

The solution is Jesus. He is life. People have a hard time choosing Him when they are only confronted by poor representations of Him.

> **Read the following verses and write down what each says regarding our speech:**
>
> **Ephesians 4:29**
>
> **Luke 6:45**
>
> **Colossians 4:6**
>
> **How might following these verses help someone see Jesus and move closer to choosing life in Him?**

As we seek to share the truth of Scripture with those with whom we may disagree, we should seek to share words of hope, forgiveness, and compassion.

> **Pray and ask God to guide your tongue and lead you to speak to others with hope, forgiveness, and compassion.**

VOICE FOR THE VOICELESS

But be doers of the word
and not hearers only,
deceiving yourselves.

JAMES 1:22

START

Welcome to the final session of *Lifemark*. Begin by reviewing the individual exercises completed by participants between group meetings.

What stood out this week in the personal studies? What truth did God reveal about what it means to shape people's views of the church and ultimately of Jesus?

Let's take some time to practice what we studied last week. Read Ephesians 4:29 aloud.

As you start this session, engage in a little group encouragement. Allow each person to take a turn celebrating or encouraging another group member. Begin each of these opportunities with the phrase, "This is how I see Jesus in you," or, "This is how I see Jesus working through you." Everyone needs encouragement and support. This is the kindness, compassion, and bearing with one another that Paul includes in his letters.

Take note of the things people say about you and soak those in for a moment. Is there anything that surprised you? Is there anything you hoped someone would notice but didn't? Is there anything you wanted to say about someone else but couldn't find the words or time ran out? Explain.

An opportunity like this doesn't have to be scripted. As you transition to the film clip portion of the study during this final gathering, make notes in the margin of anything you didn't get to say. Consider offering that up in a side conversation after group or even through an encouraging text or email later in the week. When the words are, as Ephesians 4:29 puts it, meant to build others up, they are never unwarranted.

WATCH

To access the video sessions, use the instructions at the back of your book.

View the film clip for this session together.

SUMMARY

All through the film, a secondary story is developing of characters you barely see. Nate (David's best friend) has remarked about and engaged with his sister, Reese, at various points in the story. As the movie draws to a close, Reese becomes pregnant and is considering what to do. This final clip is David's encouragement to Reese.

DISCUSS

Given the opportunity, what might you have said to Reese in this situation?

ENGAGE

Invite a group member to read James 1:22-27.

Within your personal study, you have already considered the idea that some unbelievers count hypocrisy within the church as a reason to avoid it. Engage in the following discussion with that in mind.

According to James, what does pure and undefiled religion look like?

In our context, what might James call impure and defiled religion?

How have you struggled or wavered with this idea following Jesus?

James's letter was to the twelve dispersed tribes of Jewish Christians, who had likely scattered due to intensifying persecution in the Roman Empire. This difficulty in the life of the church is the thing most attributed with the spread of the gospel throughout the world. As they fled, they took their message with them. Jewish believers, unlike Gentile converts, would have been acutely aware of the Old Testament Mosaic law and Pharisaical additions about ritualistic cleanliness and purity. James didn't write that the type of religion that is truly pure is one based on handwashing practices or ceremonial worship; he wrote that it's rooted in service and sacrifice to those who are the least.

Read Mark 9:35-37. What value did Jesus communicate in His instruction here?

In what way are Jesus's words in Mark 9 echoed in James's writing?

In Jewish social life, hospitality was a crucial value. Welcoming strangers and travelers was a supreme communal priority, so much so that references were made to all four sides of one's tent being open to welcome anyone from any direction. Jesus affirmed that welcoming a child in His name is like welcoming Him. Welcoming Him is to welcome God. In the overall biblical narrative, and particularly this word from James, orphans and widows were particularly vulnerable and Christians were specifically instructed to make room for those in need. Sometimes that means a seat at the table. Sometimes that means a word of encouragement. Sometimes that means the voice of an advocate.

You will conclude this week of personal study with reminders and creative ideas to welcome, support, and encourage others. Not only does it strengthen the body of believers when we live out this calling, but it can soften outsiders and even skeptics to the gospel. Ultimately, serving and speaking up for others in need without condemning those in crisis is how we image Jesus best.

DAY 1

UNIQUELY POSITIONED

Pastor Rick Warren writes, "Your pain often reveals God's purpose for you. God never wastes a hurt. If you have gone through a hurt, He wants you to help other people going through a similar hurt. He wants you to share it."[1]

Warren encourages people to understand that any of the problems they navigate in life can provide helpful ministry to others. Even the more shameful parts of someone's story can be leveraged to serve, support, and lead people to Jesus.

Consider the very unique place in which David found himself in this particular story. While Melissa could have offered Reese firsthand knowledge of what it is like to experience an unplanned pregnancy, to weigh your options, consider termination, and ultimately choose adoption, only David could expound firsthand the future of being spared.

In the left-hand column, make a list of a few challenges you have faced and problems you have endured or even caused in life.

Problems   Opportunities

Go back to the right column and list any opportunities those problems might afford. Perhaps you could write the name of someone you know already who is facing a similar circumstance. Perhaps it's just a potential person or situation you might be uniquely positioned to serve.

Read James 4:17 and then rewrite the verse in the space provided in your own words.

Considering the film, there would have been a time in David's life when supporting and encouraging Reese would not have been possible. At eight years old, he likely would not have possessed the wisdom, maturity, or perspective to offer words of hope. Melissa, or perhaps Susan, would have made much more likely ministers to Reese at that point.

Depending on the season, parts of your pain may be too raw. You may not be personally ready and that's okay. There may be more to work through on your end—with God and with your own support system—before you can be useful to someone else. It's important not to rush. It's important to take proper time and wait until you are ready, but it's also important to be brave and trust God for the right timing and words.

Be encouraged. God truly never wastes a hurt and can leverage absolutely everything about your life and story to gain glory and serve someone else.

James 4:17 is written at the close of a section of his letter about God's will and timing. He wrote as a warning to those who focused too much on their own plans in James 4:14: "You do not know what tomorrow will bring—what your life will be!" That's true. You don't know what tomorrow holds or who you will encounter in it. By God's divine will and His perfectly placed opportunity, you may be uniquely positioned to serve someone else with some part of your unique story.

Close by asking God to use the painful parts of your story for His greater good in the lives of others. Pray for discernment. Pray for opportunities. Pray for boldness and pray for others.

DAY 2
READY OR NOT

In *Lifemark*, there's a moment when Susan had all but given up. The pain of losing her own two sons coupled with the difficulty often associated with the adoption process led her to believe her heart just couldn't take any more grief or disappointment. She had been ready for a child but not ready for the hurt. It was overwhelming. Perhaps you have faced a similar pain or perhaps you know and love a friend or family member who has walked a difficult road with infertility, failed adoptions, or unfathomable loss.

There are so many things in life, both good and not good, that we are just never ready for, and yet God is present.

Read the following verses.

But in your hearts regard Christ the Lord as holy,
ready at any time to give a defense to anyone who asks
you for a reason for the hope that is in you.

1 PETER 3:15

But speaking the truth in love, let us grow in every way
into him who is the head—Christ.

EPHESIANS 4:15

Preach the word; be ready in season and out
of season; correct, rebuke, and encourage
with great patience and teaching.

2 TIMOTHY 4:2

What connections can you make between these three verses and your call to serve others?

When it comes to speaking up and influencing others with the truth of God's Word and love found in His gracious good news, where do you most likely fall on the following continuum?

1	2	3	4	5	6	7	8	9	10
TRUTH									LOVE
Give Answers								Gentleness/Respect	

John Stott said, "Truth without love is too hard; love without truth is too soft."[2] The unbelieving world, like Goldilocks, needs a place to rest that is neither one nor the other but the perfect blend of both. Too often, the church is perceived as a clanging gong on a street corner, screaming harshly at the world for all her wickedness. Today, it's no longer the angry street corners that we have to worry about but the social media diatribes of angry people. Conversely, the idea of softly sweeping away any talk about sin or God's sovereign rule is to kindly help people board a train headed to destruction. That's why Peter writes, "Gentleness and respect." That's why Paul exclaimed, "Truth in love."

When Susan and Jimmy get the call that a young birth mother wanted to speak to them, the actors portray so well a blend of hope and fear. When asked later, Melissa tells David, "Your parents seemed to be genuine with genuine faith." Melissa shares that she wanted a mom for David who "could have been able to do the things I would have wanted to do with you but couldn't—a mom who would be there for you and wasn't afraid to get her hands dirty."

It's easy to simply declare truth. It's messier to step into another person's story. That requires love and grace and, according to 2 Timothy 4:2, great patience.

As you close in prayer, consider memorizing the three verses from this session. Ask God to lead you to be a person who is ready to give an answer for faith, ready to stand up for the vulnerable, ready to intersect hurting people with the right blend of God's perfect truth and His abundant love.

DAY 3
REVISIT

At the conclusion of *Lifemark*, Melissa was given a token to always remember the day she chose life. She could always revisit that part of her story. As she remarked about the adoption, she shared that one literally feels every emotion. Being reminded about giving birth to David and choosing to place him in an adoptive family who could raise him meant revisiting a point of both sorrow and joy, pain and purpose. Today, as you close, take time to revisit some of the passages and concepts you engaged throughout this five-session journey.

Revisit Galatians 3:26.

If you are indeed a person of faith, one who has repented of sin and turned to Christ for forgiveness, you are an adopted son or daughter of God. That means you are His child and heir.

What does it mean to you to be God's heir? What role do you have in the world as His child?

Revisit Ephesians 1:11-13.

As a person who has received God's good gift, you are secure. You have been sealed with a promise.

What does it mean to you to be secure in faith and secure in your salvation?

What does the work of the Holy Spirit look like in your daily life? How is God moving in you to bring Himself praise and glory and accomplish His will?

Revisit Ephesians 4:32.

Kindness, compassion, and forgiveness are three character traits of God that the world desperately needs to know and understand. They are hallmarks of faith. It's God's kindness that affords salvation. It's His compassion that steps past our failure, making us candidates for His forgiveness, which affords us a place in His family.

In what ways has the forgiveness of God shaped and challenged you to extend the same to others? Are there places that you are currently withholding that you need to address? Explain.

Revisit Psalm 139:14.

God also fashioned every person. Receiving God's love and trusting His plan comes from knowing you were created with purpose.

How should your understanding of Psalm 139 shape the way you view yourself? Others who are different than you?

Revisit James 1:22.

How do you discern God's will for your life? Who has God called you to love and serve? Who has He uniquely positioned you to minister to and provide help for at this juncture in your life?

As you navigate Scripture, everything you feel, think, say, and do should be shaped by God's love for you and His desire for you to know and find joy in Him. The way you interact with the world around you, including those who are hurting and those who are actively rejecting God and His church, should be governed by what gives the greatest opportunity to speak truth, show love, and direct people to Him. This is a tall task. But as God's child and heir through Christ, it's one He chose you for and will equip you to pursue as you follow Jesus.

LEADER NOTES

GENERAL NOTE

The adoption story of David Scotton and Melissa Coles painted in the film is a best-case scenario. Adoption is always a beautiful and grace-filled process but some situations require counseling and specific help for both the adoptive parents and the children. As you celebrate God's gift of adoption and the stories of families who have walked that road, be aware that no two situations are exactly alike. However, you can be assured that if God calls you to participate in the adoption process, He will provide all that you need to make His will a reality in your life.

SESSION 1

If there is someone in your group for whom adoption is already a very personal story, invite him or her to take a few moments and share, if he or she is comfortable. Perhaps there is a group member who was adopted or is part of a family with adopted siblings. Perhaps there is a group member who has adopted or fostered a child or who is in the process of adopting. There are countless unique stories when it comes to adoption. Cherish any opportunity and encourage any participant who has experienced adoption firsthand in any way.

It's unlikely that everyone in your group lives with the blessing of a good, kind, God-honoring, earthly dad. Be sensitive as not everyone has the same experience.

SESSION 5

This is another week where sensitivity and Ephesians 4:32 kindness and tenderhearted compassion should be on display. There very well may be someone in the group whose story was marked by an unwanted teenage pregnancy. This final scene could be a trigger for those emotions regardless of the choice they made to keep or terminate. There very well may be someone else in your group walking through infertility. It is perhaps hard for them to see someone else wrestle through unwanted pregnancy when that's all they desire for themselves.

END NOTES

SESSION 2

1. The Bolt Team, "32 Cart Abandonment Statistics to Know for 2022," Bolt Financial, April 4, 2022, www.bolt.com/thinkshop/cart-abandonment-statistics-4#32-cart-abandonment-statistics.
2. "Home," Abandoned Children's Fund, accessed July 11, 2022, www.abandonedchildrensfund.org.

SESSION 3

1. The Righteous Brothers, "You've Lost That Lovin' Feelin'," Genius, accessed July 11, 2022, genius.com/The-righteous-brothers-youve-lost-that-lovin-feelin-lyrics.
2. "G863 - aphiēmi - Strong's Greek Lexicon (kjv)." Blue Letter Bible, accessed July 21, 2022, www.blueletterbible.org/lexicon/g863/kjv/tr/0-1/.

SESSION 5

1. Czarina Ong, "Pastor Rick Warren Explains Why Pain Is Essential in One's Life: It 'Reveals God's Purpose for You,'" Christian Today, November 8, 2016, www.christiantoday.com/article/pastor-rick-warren-explains-why-pain-is-essential-in-ones-life-it-reveals-gods-purpose-for-you/100023.htm.
2. "John R. W. Stott Quotes," quotefancy, accessed July 11, 2022, www.quotefancy.com/quote/1432400John-R-W-Stott-Truth-without-love-is-too-hard-love-without-truth-is-too-soft.

WHAT DO
YOU ALLOW
TO DEFINE
YOU?

FROM THE CREATORS OF WAR ROOM

OVERCOMER

This five-session small group Bible study uses clips from the film *OVERCOMER* to examine how we determine our identity and how we can find our true identity in Christ.

Learn more about this Bible study at lifeway.com/overcomerbiblestudy and more about the *OVERCOMER* movie and products at lifeway.com/overcomer.

Lifeway